JESUS Is The Reason For The Season

a collection of poems for God's glory alone.

by Fergus Richard Davar

BookLeaf Publishing
India | USA | UK

Made with ❤ on the BookLeaf Publishing Platform
www.bookleafpub.in
www.bookleafpub.com

DEDICATION

This collection of poems is dedicated to
my Lord, God, & Saviour, Jesus Christ,
who has seen me through thick & thin.
When my family and friends forsook me,
He was there for me. I have but one life,
and that, I shall live for His glory.

So help me, God!

ACKNOWLEDGEMENT

I would like to thank a few people who have shown me kindness and supported me in their own capacity, through my life. May God bless them in His love.

1. My mum— Priscilla Philomena Davar, whom I love dearly.
2. The cops at Tilak Nagar Police Station (Mumbai), who have supported me against various hateful, anti-social elements, including my biological father.
3. My ex-bosses at work viz. Latesh, Vandana, Suresh, Arnobi, Biswajit, Ravi, Pat, and Harshad, whose love & support in their own capacity, has been a conduit of God's blessing in my life.

Preface

This collection of inspired poem is a foretaste of what it is like to have God by your side, as you are honed to be his instrument of righteousness in a dark world that loves sin, and while the world may ponder and even ask why God chose me for the task He has given me, the truth is I don't know the answer myself. I hate the attention, but I love Jesus more than I love myself. So I have counted the cost, knowing I have nothing more than my life to pay, for bearing witness to the truth... which I have expressed in this collection of poems.

Only those whose lives God is working in, can appreciate truth the Bible says in Phil 1:6 & 1Cor 2:14, while the rest of the world prefers the flattery of lies. So, if you don't enjoy content that takes your eyes off yourself and focuses them on the Lord Jesus Christ, who deserves your adoration & worship, I get it. You might not enjoy what's within these pages.

Index

A Christmas Poem

Writing for Christmas, this is my first
attempt,
Last year came and went,
& I did not even a finger bend.

Now I am saved
& I am learning to behave.
Christmas is the only time I do not complain
about having a shave.

I've heard some on Christmas preach,
I wonder if they follow what they teach.
They said Christmas is not about parties or
the clothes you wear,
It is about the heart, care, and share.
That was only politically correct, for my ears
to bear.
There was very little Jesus, which now causes
my heart to tear.

When a man has a son or daughter,
He celebrates with everyone but rarely with
God who brought him or brought her.

With Christmas, what is similar?
Places are lit with lights of every colour.
Yeah, celebration is great, I love it,
But how can we celebrate when we forget
how we got it?

Christmas is not about Santa,
A man in red, as fat as a panda.

So is it the Snowman?

NO... there's got to be more MAN.

What about Christmas trees?
They're Pretty,
Nope, there is a lot more to Christmas...
PLEASE.

What about Rudolf? Or Santa's elves?
Or Christmas candles or Christmas bells?
Don't tell me that is where your mind on
Christmas dwells,
The Samaritan woman learned more when
she met Jesus at the well.

So why do we celebrate Christmas? What is
the reason?
The answer is Jesus, all through the season.
You'll ask about Jesus, what is so great?
Just think, God came to free man of the sins
man made.

One of the many things that makes the
Gospel come alive,
Is God-the-Father, before the world's
creation, His Son glorified,

That is what is written in John 17:five,
Before all creation, Jesus was Almighty,
Sovereign & High.

From the beginning to the end,
The Father, Jesus & Holy Spirit are Sovereign.
You can check that in Revelation 22:(3 + ten).
When man is born, man has a celebration,
When God was as man born, all rejoiced in all
creation,
Because then came my Lord, my lone
Salvation.

Rejoice and be glad,
His birth as man, is what made Satan mad.
If you were in prison and then set free,
How happy would you be?
From the bondage of death, Jesus gives
victory,
If you trusted Him, you'd be happy,
Very happy.

So remember, Christmas is all abuzz,
& only about the One who came to save us.

Just as hostages are overwhelmed with tears
by their rescue,
May His Spirit touch you, even if you are at a
party barbecue.

So let us rejoice, heaven and earth,
In our Hero, whose side was pierced.
Out of humility and grace, He came as man,
On that Judgment day, deny Him as Lord &
Savior... no one can.

So this Christmas, let us come together and
celebrate,
Partying and praising Jesus' name, as that's
what the Father appreciates.
& I close this poem wishing Merry Christmas
to all my mates.

Superstition Vs Obedience to God

Superstition comes about
When people love themselves first,
Resorting to silliness like zodiac signs,
& crossing before the cat crosses the road.
Still, their believing in themselves
Never satisfies them or quenches their thirst.

Biblical Christianity,
On the other hand,
Is about resting your faith in God
& walking in obedience
Despite the odds.

The wages of sin is death,
And it is better to refrain from sin
Than to not walk under the ladder
Or race the cat on the road & win.

When you prize truth over yourself,
You somehow gain common sense,
& do away with all forms of demonic
divination,
Including astrology, palmistry, & kundli etc.
Which is nothing short of nonsense.

Many foolishly
Love themselves first, & above all,
Like they're their own god,
A lie sold to mankind from the fall.
Then they naturally go about life,
Like they have neither sense, nor balls.

It is written,
The fool says in his heart,
There is no God.
Because whether a young coon,
Or an old fart,

Unbelievers live selfishly,
Sucking up to others,
While thinking they are different,
A people set apart.

Wise in their own eyes, are unbelievers,
Who judge others,
Without first looking in the mirror!
It's no wonder superstition is the way
For these counterfeit gods & selfish fools,
Who will have nothing but hell to pay.

So, get over yourselves
& believe in Jesus.
Only then you can quit
All this superstitious silliness.

Between God & Man

There are times man ponders on himself,
That had he not existed,
Would anything matter to himself?

So, as he sees himself as the center in all he knows,
He thinks he himself is god,
And that's the way the world goes,
For had he not existed, would anything matter to
him so?

But how can that which comes to being be
self-existent?
Or how that which grows, be Omnipotent?
Can that which is learning, say it knows all
things?
When, as life goes on, it the unknown brings!

Satan was probably the first who sought to be God,
Until he was smitten by Jesse's Rod.
God is a Jealous God, and tolerates no rivals,
And even the spirit of the anti-Christ serves His purpose in denial.
As all things are created to meet a certain purpose of His,
Which even Satan fulfills, as much in betrayal as in Judas' kiss.

Man can never become God, though God became man,
For as long as man is learning or growing, become God, he never can.
But when man is convinced he knows all,
What awaits this god is only downfall.

In Christ, the fullness of His eternal Father dwelled,
But as a man, His meekness meant His head never swelled.
He dealt harshly with hypocritical power,
And to the bruised reed, He was their Strong tower.

So, fellow man, if it's you and not Christ, around whom you center,
Then the fire you'll inherit will strike faster than the colour magenta.

Total Depravity!

When I approach His throne of grace,
The stench of my being fills my face.
I feel so strongly to glorify His Name,
What contrast! His glory is to my shame!

By myself, I pay trespass for trespass,
But it's out of His goodness that I continue to last.
My sin is like my bed, upon which I rest,
And this I cover with pride, way over my head
and chest.

Things sometimes feel like they can't get any
worse,
& then I do something to give into my desire's
thirst.
His Spirit counsels me to quieten my rebelling,
But I am a victim of feelings, consuming but
never fulfilling.

While Satan's bastards judge me,
Wanting to take out the speck,
So I can better see.
These syndicates of shit,
Have been hating me secretly.
Earning karma, just as they befit;
& as they pretend all is well,
They are on Highway to Hell.

Yes, of myself, I have little control.
After the relationships they've sabotaged,
And accuse me of having ravaged,
But by His goodness, I am still on parole.
May God all these haters damn,
India, false friends, & Mel Everingham.

God, in His goodness, is always Sovereign!
And He converts to life hearts solid and frozen.
So, when I look in worship into His marvelous
face,
I am reminded of my depraved and sinful distaste.
& also all those haters who tried to lay me to
waste.

Yes, I have sinfully sought many a other pleasure,
When Christ ought to be my first and only
treasure.

But God has used many spiritual degenerates,
To sanctify me and of my salvation reassure.
As assuredly as I have life, I know of His providence,
And when He decrees, I shall take every thought captive to Him in obedience.

This piece of my life is the painful part of His threshing,
Where what is born of His Spirit is the wheat in me beginning.
And my mutinies are like the dead chaff painfully dwindling.
For I am a member of His Church, aka Israel in the making,
Overcoming a world of haters by Jesus gracious saving.

So, I pray to my loving God-the-Father,
That I may hold fast to my faith
In His Son Jesus Christ, and no other,
May God-the-Holy-Spirit sanctify me
Through the saving blood of my Firstborn Brother.

Our Sovereign God

Where most people in this world blink,
Is in the thought that God only knows many a thing.
They seem to find it hard to think,
That God even decrees the actions of their sins that stink.

If you were to ask: Would God decree that what He speaks against?
Think then of the Pharaoh who kept His people as slaves fenced.
Did God not ask Pharaoh to let His people go?
Yet He made Pharaoh stubborn, to make known His All-Might so.

This Pharaoh did to His people all things of gory,
And then God's justice brought down
This mighty nation to the state of sorry.
So there you have it all in one story,
That God does all things for His own glory.

Now, for those whose minds are a little curious,
May wonder, is it therefore okay to do things with intention spurious,
For if all things are his will,
Then how can it ever make Him furious?

Do you know the time when Jesus was tempted?
Satan told Him something scripturally demented.
For scripture stated that if He plummeted from that huge height,
God's will would ensure His angels upheld Him, that His foot may not be hurt, even slight.

So, what did Jesus have to say to that Satan of
a pest?
He said, for scripture says- You shall not put
God to the test.

So my friend, if you are a believer,
Then know that from God,
We are just of mercy a receiver.
God loves Himself and He has full right,
For besides Father, Son, and Holy Spirit.
There is no perfect being in sight.
So let's not blasphemously of Godly equality
speak,
But give Him that deserving worship, He has
taught us to seek.

Design-perfect Chaos

Why is it that man is hassled by chaos?
It is because he prefers life to be served to him,
Like it were all available at a kiosk.
What is 'chaos' in a person's mind?
It's having as much control on life,
As a man who walks, though he is blind!

It's like when you step into a fish market,
You can't decipher who is saying what and to whom.
You've come by car when there is no place to park it!
So what is all this?

It is about us who love control,
Told we are mere stewards in a world, that is
His!

Since the fall of Adam in the garden,
Man received his own standard of
righteousness.
This was separate from God and without
pardon!
Adam's falls has changed our perspective of
life,
Where what we cannot control, we despise,
As righteousness is now each one's own,
towards eternal strife.

So chaos truly,
is because man is unruly!

Man, from His fall, is crippled,
And so such a thing as trusting God,
Makes man think that his strife would be
tripled.
Ideally, there is no such thing as chaos,
But man disbelieves God controls all,

As fall's sting leaves man dumbfounded like a sea horse.

This is the break from the rat race,
Every natural man runs,
As though it were keeping up with life's pace!
To believe in one's heart that God controls all,
Requires man to put away pride
And admit his folly, from mankind's fall.

Life is not for man to control,
And to even desire such a thing,
Shows man is, since Adam, a depraved being on the roll.
A man's desire to control every outcome,
Shows his broken communion with God,
Who is infinitely beyond all creation,
Even if all were put together in total sum!

If you asked: How much better,
Are the works of God as compared to men?
Then view the detail in a thread of a sweater!
& then take a look at blood under a microscope,

And you see! The perfect design of an RBC!
While a thread appears as a chaotic
kaleidoscope!

Man may believe only in what he sees,
So chaos is man's incapacity to look beyond
himself,
And see Almighty God working all things to
the 'T'.
Even if a person completed his doctorate with
a brilliant thesis,
He still misses out on a rich relationship with
God,
If this person knows not the Lord Jesus!

Like a person sitting pillion on a motorcycle,
Who barely trust the rider,
Such a person is worried sick,
Even when the engine is running idle,
So also it is with us men naturally,
Who trust not God,
But trust men, instead of God, fearfully!

So, I close by inviting every person to
remember,

That one need not substitute God's solutions in the Bible,
For there is blessing in obeying His Law from January to December!
His Moral Law commands you to first to love God above all,
& second, to love your neighbour as yourself.

I Stand Slandered

I grew up being told
I was the cause of all the fights in the house,
Called a parasite, leper, good-for-nothing —a
liability
But I didn't turn out a church mouse;
I don't stand corrected but slandered.

When I came to faith,
What surfaced in my friends was hate.
Time after time, I was betrayed
& then deemed a mental case.
I don't stand corrected but slandered.

In most of my jobs, I was thrown out.
I worked sincerely till I was worn out,
Still, they never failed to find fault,
Because my faith influenced the
environment like salt.
I don't stand corrected but slandered.

All my relationships were sabotaged
By fakers whom even God detests,
And when I kept my distance,
I was labelled a woman-hater & sexist.
I don't stand corrected but slandered.

Out on the road I have no rest,
As people just couldn't care less.
Carts, cycles, scooters, motorbikes rickshaws &
cars
All these prepare a show for me from afar
From stalling me,
To mocking me,
To running into me,
To showing me money & friends I haven't got.
These unbelievers are a ridiculous lot
I don't stand corrected but slandered.

Even in church, I'm not spared.
So much for pastors
Who don't really care.
From ill advice to secret plots,
The truth isn't something
these goats have got.
I don't stand corrected but slandered.

I am told to be first Indian

& then Christian,
By people who spit, steal & litter.
But India isn't greater than my Lord Jesus—
That truth is indeed bitter
I don't stand corrected but slandered.

I have paid for services I didn't get
& have even threatened with arrest,
By my parents, people on the road,
& a bank manager too.
But if I am important,
Why should I bow to the likes of you?
& if I am a nobody,
Why hate me the way you do?
I don't stand corrected but slandered.

After all is said and done,
I have counted the cost,
& Jesus is worthy,
While Satan's bastards get lost
In God's Judgement, as their karma deems
worthy.
Like their father who roamed aimlessly in Job 1,
All their relationships are time pass,
As they only love themselves & no one.
I don't stand corrected but slandered.

Jesus, A Friend You Can Trust!

In a world where people
Look for friends with stuff,
Few look for friends
They can trust!

A friend to all
Is a friend to none, they say,
But Jesus is one dude
Who will fight them all for you.
Read Daniel 10:13 to 21!
If there is One guy you can trust,
The Lord Christ is the only One, you must.

And so if love has anything
To do with trust,
Surely, loving Jesus first
Is a must,
Because there is none better
In whom you can trust.

Yes, Jesus is for real.
No wonder the thought of Him
Makes even demons shudder.
...because He has destined
Even the god of this world
To be hell's fodder.

Covetousness allows fake people
To exploit their family & friends.
But Jesus is that One friend
Who is there with this people
Till the very end.

So, for those who don't say of the Lord,
"Jesus hai mera dost, mera bundha,"
In hell you will burn as you deserve
& get the damn dunda.

Self-idolatry Vs Christianity

There are 2 types of people, essentially:
Those who love Christ first,
& those who love themselves first.
The latter are troublemakers, & Satan's bastards.
While the former live quietly for God's glory.

Surely you have noticed how selfish people,
Are so helpless.
Their presence spiritually pollutes the land,
Being estranged from God & His commands.

Like a Bollywood film,
Their lives are far from reality.

And their emotions aren't prudent
But all over the place like loose motions

Their love is based on neither truth nor trust,
Because these bastards of Satan,
Are always loving themselves first.

Like India that fought for Pakistan,
Successfully For Bangladesh, Not PoK,
To Kiss Arab Butt.
Their loving themselves first,
Allows them to use & abuse,
As they are cowards with no guts.

Unlike Biblical Christianity ,
Where you love your neighbour,
As yourself.
Self-idolators love their neighbour,
Only for themselves.
Hence, their products & services
Show their fire burns,
Not in their stomach,
But in their butt.

Their hatred for us,

Comes from their hatred of truth.
For their names aren't in His book,
And at the gate, they will be told...
"Chal fut!"

Faith Vs Fate

Ever noticed how those
who live a carefree life
Say, "Life is a bitch,"
After chasing after,
Selfish pleasure.
They found themselves,
In a ditch.

Yet, these haven't learnt their lesson,
& like typical heathens,
They chase after their own passions.

These are the fools for Psalm 14:1,
Who say in their hearts,
"There is no God,"

As they live a lie,
In living selfishly for themselves,
Like a bunch of sods.

As opposed to these mentioned above,
There are those who live by faith.
These are Christ's followers aka Christians,
Who are born from above.

We walk by faith,
Not by sight,
And so we fight for what is right.
For the joy of God,
Is our might.

Unlike the damn heathen,
Who love themselves first,
We love Jesus first,
& endure hardship
In a world of sin.
Because we know,
In Christ, we win!

So, unlike the hangovers
These heathen suffer,

A taste of khud-khushi,
Our joy knows no bound.
For our faith rest in Jesus,
Who's good, like delicious sushi.

God's Faithfulness, Reflected In "dog"

Like the moon reflects
The light of the sun,
The faithfulness of God
Is reflected in a dog.

Like a laterally reversed image,
Where you can read in the mirror,
The word "AMBULANCE".
The faithfulness of a dog,
Says Christ second coming,
Will be of glorious magnificence

In world that praises itself,

The story of the Canaanite woman,
Is one of true prostration & obedience.
A reflection of His faithfulness
to the very end.
A faithfulness Jesus Himself praised,
For we are made in His image,
& His glorious presence,
Is our joy and blessed resonance.

It was John Calvin, who said,
"I'd be a coward,
If I said nothing when
The truth is compromised,
Because even a dog barks
When his master is attacked."
The faithfulness of a dog, therefore,
Comes as no surprise.

Remember, dogs have come from wolves,
& Jesus did say "He who is forgiven more,
Loves more and lives by God's rules."
Though we may be gentiles,
But the love for the Lord our God Jesus
Christ,
In our blood, runs wild.

The vision of Peter in Acts 10
Is more that just of dietary cleansing—
It is the wild olive branch
grafted to a cultivated olive branch.

In this, we are catholic,
That we who aren't one in blood
Are one in His Spirit.
Like those beasts with divided hooves,
We are from the world but called apart,
To meditate on His word,
like beasts who chew the cud.

We are one body,
& one Spirit in Christ.
& may the Lord grant us that strength,
That, for His glory, if we must,
Even risk our lives
Because Jesus is worthy.

Biblical Christianity
Is Transforming The World

The Bible says in James 1:27,
True religion is about caring
For widows & orphans.
Not so long ago,
Hindus burnt their widows in Sati,
& adoption in Islam is still forbidden.

Not so long ago,
Masons were murdered
After building monuments.
Being skilled was a curse.
Still, the Bible pioneered

Rescuing the Hebrews,
who build the pyramids
From Egyptian slave drivers
Who were far worse.

Not so long ago,
What we have now as prisons,
Were formerly dungeons,
A pagan form of captivity & brutality,
Which the Bible sees as human depravity.
As freedom is at the heart
Of Biblical Christianity.
Punishments up to Capital punishment
Or recompensing victims for their loss,
Depending on the heinousness of crime
Is Biblical practicality.

Not so long ago
The leftist KKK deemed
The Negro was not human.
Hitler's leftist Nazi regime
Thought the same of the Jews too.
It was Christian right wingers,
Who though few,
sheltered the Jews,

& in the US fought for negro rights too,
Because every human is made in God's image.
And cannot be treated like filthy garbage.

Even today,
The world bows where they get kicked,
While tyrants enjoy getting their butts licked.
But the Bible teaches
To resist the devil & submit to God,
Not rarely but oft,
Which tells Satan to sod-off.

Even today,
In a world of self-loving wussies.
We Christians are obedient sheep.
Our wisdom comes from our fear of God,
Like still & quiet waters that run deep.

Even today,
Haters hate on us & senselessly judge,
But we love Jesus more than dear life,
So we will do what is right
And so no, we won't bow or budge.

Not so long ago,

The martyred Saint-
Graham Staines
picked up & treated lepers.
Not caring of how his own image would sink.
Cause we put our hand to the plough,
Like it were divine instinct.
For we aren't god to ourselves,
We're only concerned with what Jesus thinks.

His knowledge will fill the earth,
This God has promised
In Habakuk 2 verse 14.
Though Satan & the power of sin in the world
May be great,
God is greater,
& in Jesus we overcome the world, times
umpteen.

Say No To Abortion.
Say Yes To Life.

Did you know,
Only about 1% of the unborn aborted
Are conceived from rape?
The rest simply want to live carefree
& without responsibility.

Why should someone pay with their life,
For your life of pleasure?
You have no right to destroy
That which God knits in your womb,
Like it were a treasure.

Though you may be the prettiest,

If you support abortion,
Spiritually, you are ugly.
Far worse than even murderous terrorists.
They may rip people apart with bombs.
But you rip apart,
The innocent child of your womb.

While terrorists kill about 30 thousand
people,
In massacres around the world,
Abortion slaughters about 73 million unborn,
by physically very pretty girls.
If terrorism is condemned,
So must abortion,
& you didn't even bother to use,
A damn condom.

Abortion is condoned,
Because, in a world
That loves itself first,
Someone else paying
With their lives,
Even if they be your own kids.
For your carefree life,
Is murder justified.

You may be pretty on the outside, woman,
But on the inside,
You are far uglier than those terrorists, who
are far gone.

Say no to abortion.
Say yes to life!
Happiness begins,
With being a faithful wife.

Sinful Pride
Vs Godly Pride

The world may support the LGBTQ
And Rapists & Pedophiles too.
With child sex-trafficking,
And letting rapists live,
Because to be at world's mercy,
Is to know they have nothing,
But hell to give.

The hedonistic life,
Is one of self-indulgence,
& self-pleasure.
But did you know,

Karma is no butt-kisser,
And khud-khushi is suicide,
Because if you aren't on God's side,
You are on a road,
That will take your own life.

The world may support you,
In hating God with your sin.
But good eventually wins,
& only Jesus can save you from yourself.

So, if the Lord so wills,
I pray that you repent & believe the Gospel-
You cannot be right, when you are wrong,
You silly damn ding-dong.
Just because every liar tells you so.
Open your eyes,
You are wrong,
God is right.

Seek the Lord,
And make His joy your might.
And take pride & enjoy
Fighting the good fight.

So, don’t settle for that
Victim mentality & sad stories.
Live life, alive and kicking,
Fight the good fight,
All for Jesus' glory.

Born From Above

Like the movie *Phenomenon*,
Where JT gets hit by light,
Which changes his whole life,
My life changed drastically too.

The Bible says God uses fools
To mock the wisdom of the world,
And, through us, display His might.
Why God chooses us, I don't know.
There is nothing special in us.
But His choosing us makes us special
To bear witness to Him, on the go.

Like in the *War Robots* video game,

Where legendary pilots make all the
difference.
His spirit works in us
for the glory of Jesus's name.
For God is gracious, & God is good.
And like the late Saint- Graham Staines,
Who carried lepers around,
His infectious grace carries us around,
Unclean sinners, who are sinfully bound.

The Bible says that, while we were still
sinners,
Christ died for us.
In Him, despite every tribulation,
We are overcomer & are winners.

This spiritual rebirth
Isn't something we deserve.
It is by grace, unmerited favour.

So, like the battery: *Amaron*,
that lasts long, really long, ting tong.
I, who was once a damn ding-dong,
Am evidence Jesus is for real.
In Him, I overcome every trial.

Though I am but a gentile,
It's by Christ's infinite worth,
I am graciously counted as one,
Among His sheep, aka Israel.

God is Good & Jesus is Worthy

Everyone believes God is Great.
It is only Christianity,
That essentially says... God is good.
Which is why the Bible says...
Taste & see, the Lord is good.
Because when you eat good food.
You can't help but think... God is good.

While self-idolators,
like cats, might think: "God feeds me,
Clothes me, and cares for me
I'm so important."

True Christians are as that
Canaanite woman
Whom Jesus called a
Woman of great faith.
Because, like dogs,
When we are fed,
Clothed, cared for,
And loved, we know
Jesus is worthy.

Though the world may deny us,
Any credit for our labour!
We wait on the Lord,
And renew our strength.
To Him, and Him alone be the glory.
Psalm 115:1
Apologetics doesn't mean we are sorry.
It's all about fighting the good fight,
And living for Jesus' glory.

Our strength knows no limit,
Because the joy of the Lord
Is our open secret.
We are not cats.
Not self-idolators.

Not unbelievers.
We are Christians!
& though none may stand by us,
We shall stand by Jesus,
As He stands by us.
We are not ashamed of the truth.
We may not have it all together,
But God does, and God is good.

So no matter how much,
We get tanned.
Jesus is worthy, &
We are in good hands.

The World Denies Whom God Accepts

Like a jealous husband,
Is the Lord Jesus Christ.
In His sovereignty,
The world rejects
Whom God loves,
Because the grapes are sour.
For Christ is their Lord,
Not their Saviour,
As He is ours.

They can't and will never steal His thunder.

For whom God has destined for honour,
The world can't help but dishonour.
Better still, in this severe treatment,
As with Shadrach, Meshach, & Abednego,
Jesus is our first-born brother.

The world likes to play the fool
And so deject,
Where they themselves are rejects.
Because these are gods to themselves,
In their own eyes.
Worshiping themselves,
with a weaponry of lies.

If everyone lies, it doesn't become truth,
As false prophets unite people in neither truth nor love.
They are but... *kabab me huddees*,
Known by the fruit!

All is not well,
As these are headed to hell.
Truth is not what they make-believe.
Truth is what has them on pins.
The god of this world is judged,

But the truth of God,
Which is Jesus, won’t budge.

Let's leave these unbelievers
In a huff.
Don't ever believe in yourself.
Put your faith in Jesus Christ,
& call their damn bluff.

God's Salvation Is By Election

Yes, true religion isn't of man's choosing.
Unlike those enforced by man's abusing.

Under every Church steeple,
Bible-believing Christians learn:
It is God who chooses His people.
And so Christian culture is fruitful.
As we don't convert people under duress,
For predestination allows us to be peaceful.

The British ruled India,
China, and most of the Middle-east,
For centuries.
Yet there was no significant conversion

Of the people to Christianity.
To force our religion on others is odd,
& it is not the way of our one true Triune
God.

Unlike the Hindu's *Ghar Wapsi*, which
towered
When the BJP, in 2014, came to power,
Where thousands of tribals
Who converted to Christianity
Were brought back to Hinduism.
After being physically harmed
& accosted with profanity!

Unlike the Jihad of Islam,
Where their hatred for truth & life is
enkindled.
To see the number of Jews, Christians, and
Yazidis
In the Middle-East to dwindle.

Unlike China too, where Christians pay the
price.
As leaders enforce new laws, where Christian
converts

Must donate their kids to Buddhist temples,
As a penalty for coming to faith in Christ.

So, unlike these tyrannical, man-enforced religions,
Like Islam, Hinduism, and Buddhism,
In Christianity, despite the hateful slander,
There is no forced conversion.

From John 1 verses 12 to 13 & Daniel 2 verse 44 to 45
We know, no man has a hand,
In Christ's wedding band.
As the onus of genuine faith,
Rests on God alone who saves.
Not on man, who is insecure & depraved.

Unlike unbelieving tyrants who impose their faith,
From insecurity & a guilt triggered conscience.
Without giving any ear to even common sense.
We Christians, though slandered & against all odds,

Don’t think of ourselves as gods.
We choose self-respect over being selfish.
As our faith is unlocked,
When we live for the Lord,
Christ-centered lives, that are selfless.

In nature itself we see,
what's called natural selection.
As nature glorifies its Maker,
who establishes the Christian faith,
By way of election.

Son-kissed Vs Butt-kissed
FAITH

What distinguishes believers from unbelievers
Is the faith that moves mountains,
As if it were a lever.

Hence, unbelieving India,
Could not fight Pakistan for PoK,
For over 70 years.
As it liberated Bangladesh in a year,
Like unbelievers who know no better
Trading their self-respect,
For selfishness, like sluts.

Cause unlike the 1971 Bangladesh war,
PoK could not be fought for,
By kissing Arab butt.

Yes, unbelievers kiss the butts
of the who's who,
In serving their own vested interest.
Hence their nature has that
typical stench of ghu ghu.
As they kiss butt in trading
Their self-respect for selfishness.

Biblical Christianity on the other hand,
Isn't about pleasing others,
Motivated by selfish interest.
It's about pleasing God to serve God.
Because we are not spiritually twisted.
This Psalm 2 calls...
Kissing God-the-Son in worship.
Which all together describes,
True Christian character & fellowship.

Unlike self-centered unbelievers,
who aren't concerned about people.
But only about what people think of 'em.
Christ-centered believers,
Are concerned for their neighbour
& never bothered, of what others think of them.

For while unbelievers live,
A life full of drama for themselves,
As though their spirits were spiked.
Believers live for that one audience,
Who saves us from sin & hell,
aka the Lord Jesus Christ.

The One true Triune God

While scoffers mock the Holy Trinity,
They fail to see the Holy Unity,
Of God-the-Father, God-the-Son, &
God-the-Holy-Spirit,
Who are individually unique & yet One.
& it is their unity that defines,
That God is relational & God is love,
In believers, who are born from above.

The uniqueness of Biblical Christianity is
enamored,
In that God judges with his own character as
His standard.

Hence, Jesus prayed that we Christians would be one,
Just as God-the-Father is one with God-the-Son.

In Hindi there is a idiom-
"Samajdar ko ishara kafi hai."
So also, the Bible wasn't written,
For those who are stupid and dumb.

Like some things understood
From an unspoken picture,
The concept of the Holy Trinity
Is implicitly taught, though not
Explicitly mentioned in scripture.

If you look at the Great Commission
In Mat 28:18 to 20.
We see mention of God who is Triune,
Here and in other places too, aplenty.
Evidence from Colossians 1 & Genesis 1 too surmounts,
Revealing God's Triune nature in the creation account.
While Psalm 2 & John 1

Are dedicated to revealing God-the-Son

Like a family of different unique entities,
But of one surname and stock-head.
The Father, Son, and Holy Spirit are unique
Representing YHWH as one Godhead.

The Father, Son, and Holy Spirit,
In creation and redemption,
Are co-equal but serve different roles.
Just like a ship that leaves the shore.
Going from the drawing board
To being built in the dock,
& setting sail in the sea:
God-the-Father plans,
God-the-Son materializes that plan,
& God-the-Holy-Spirit gets it rolling,
You see!

Sorry Jesus.
Thank You Jesus.

In a world where each are,
gods to themselves.
People don't apologize,
Even when they are wrong.
Because they are *bhagwans*,
& these damn ding dongs.
Neither show no appreciation
When people do them good.
Because they are *bhagwans* again,
Ungratefully seeking after selfish gain.

Coming to faith, however,
Can never be too late.
In this, we truly prostrate,
Like it were a spiritual realization,
That gets us off our selfish fixation.
Being never grateful and never sorry.
Is like going through life like dead bodies.
With stone hearts & a seared conscience,
Unbelievers love themselves first,
As it justifies their jealousy, hatred,
& a whole lot of other nonsense.

To repent & believe the Gospel,
Is simply this-
That you die to yourself,
Live for the Lord Jesus.
For you are not your own but His.
Because, did you know,
People who commit suicide,
All burn in hell.
That itself should tell you,
You are not a god to yourself.

To love yourself first,

Is to hate truth.
Honestly self-introspect &
You will see the rotten fruit.
Because you unbelievers,
Are all living a lie.
& that is no way
Anyone should die.

David said in the Psalms...
"Against You Alone God, Have I Sinned!"
Because no matter what he did,
Everyone blindly accepted him.
Love is blind!
When you love anything but Jesus first.
Yes, all you self-idolators
In one way or another,
Are out of your damn minds.

So, I pray you summon the courage,
And apologize to Jesus for a life of sin.
& then thank Him, for in His death &
resurrection,
We overcome our sin & win.

www.ingramcontent.com/pod-product-compliance
Lightning Source LLC
Chambersburg PA
CBHW051734130826
49812CB00033B/857
9789367398173